CONTEMPORARY KITCHENS

BETA-PLUS

CONTEMPORARY KITCHENS

p. 2
A Wilfra ID&E
kitchen design.

p. 4-5
A Mape project.

January 2007
ISBN 13: 978 90 772 1371 1
ISBN 10: 90 772 1371 6

CONTENTS

FOREWORD

For the first time in this home-design series, we are devoting an entire volume to contemporary kitchen creations.

This completely new publication (2007-2008) features the latest kitchen projects by leading designers and kitchen manufacturers.

A great deal of attention is also devoted to high-quality kitchen equipment, such as exclusive cookers, hobs and large refrigerators.

Contemporary kitchens have undergone a real transformation in recent years.
What was once a purely functional space has developed into a proper living environment, which is still used for cooking, but also for eating, watching TV, and even as an informal place to receive guests.

The kitchen has grown to accommodate these developments. The space itself has become larger and additional elements have been added, such as dining tables, breakfast bars, TV screens and fireplaces.
Technological innovations and sophisticated kitchen equipment are now being integrated into complete concepts, with other interior elements also playing an important role: lighting, colour palette, materials, and all of the other features that make an interior into a pleasant living environment.

Wim Pauwels
Publisher

A Strato project.

p. 12-13
A kitchen design by
Stephanie Laporte,
handmade by Obumex.

PART I

INSPIRING PROJECTS BY LEADING KITCHEN DESIGNERS

ALL IN ONE: KITCHEN, LIBRARY, DINING AND LIVING ROOM

This report illustrates the architect's mission to bring a 1960s house into line with modern living and working habits, whilst, as far as possible, retaining the original volumes and architecture.

The divisions between the different rooms within the space have been removed, improving the circulation throughout the house.

One large space was created over the entire length of the house so as to incorporate the garden into the living area. This space contains the dining room, kitchen, living room and library.

The offices have been situated along the side of the house facing the street, creating a good division between work and private life.

A view of the newly created dining room with the long table and gas fire as central elements.

p. 18
The open kitchen reveals the architect's aim: a symbiosis of functionality, user-friendliness and comfort.
The warmth of the wood contrasts with the cool stone and marble.
The stainless-steel appliances harmonise by adopting the tones of their surroundings.

Above
There is storage space in the wall cupboards and in the drawers of the central unit. This keeps the atmosphere calm and streamlined.

Left
The central unit has a surface in the darkest available type of granite, with a soft sheen. The drawers of the unit provide ample storage space.

p. 20-21
A view of the kitchen and dining room, as seen from the living room.
The table and the cupboard units beside the fireplace are custom-made.
The table forms the central visual point of the dining area.

VAN RAVESTYN bvba
Architectural studio
    Kastelein 70
    B – 2300 Turnhout
    T +32 (0)14 42 77 41
    F +32 (0)14 43 77 44
    www.vanravestyn.be
    info@vanravestyn.be

LIGHT AND OPENNESS

The key feature of this kitchen and dining area, designed by architect Baudouin Courtens, is the long window, an opening to the outside.

With large window sections on three sides, the kitchen looks out onto the garden and onto the covered terrace on the ground floor.

In this kitchen, fine materials have been combined with natural shades.

The floors have been laid with lava stone and the work surfaces are in Zimbabwe natural stone.

The kitchen furniture, all of which was designed by the architect, has been coloured to tone with the finish of the exterior walls.

The central unit is in tinted, brushed oak.

BAUDOUIN COURTENS
Architectural studio
    av. Napoléon 152/2
    B – 1180 Brussels
    T +32 (0)2 375 35 12
    F +32 (0)2 375 29 41
    www.courtens.be
    bc@courtens.be

Particular attention has been paid to the lights. Most of the lighting is indirect, accentuating the effect of the lowered ceiling section that contains the extractor unit.

EXCLUSIVE, CONTEMPORARY KITCHENS TAILORED TO THE CLIENT'S NEEDS

Paul van de Kooi creates top-quality kitchens completely to the specifications and wishes of the client.

Whether the project involves a classic country kitchen or a more contemporary look, every project by Paul van de Kooi Kitchens is characterised by the constant pursuit of the ultimate in quality and the exclusive use of high-quality materials that are processed by experienced professionals.

The four contemporary kitchen designs that are presented in this report perfectly demonstrate the skill of this renowned kitchen designer.
The customer can find further inspiration in the company's showroom in Amersfoort, where there are always around fifteen exclusive kitchens on display.

The work surface was cast in concrete on-site.

The interiors of the cupboards are in glued birch multiplex; the façades are in three-layer oak laminate.

The Viking cooker is 92 cm wide. Miele (high-pressure) steam oven and a combi-oven, also by Miele. The extraction system is by Itho.

The Viking cooker is 122 cm wide. The existing chimney above has been converted into a cooker hood. Cupboard interiors in glued birch multiplex; façades and sides in solid afrormosia wood. A Gaggenau steam oven and a Viking fridge-freezer combination (width: 122 cm).

The kitchen work surface is in Nero Assoluto natural stone with a smoothed finish.

This kitchen was conceived by the well-known designer Marcel Wolterinck and created by Paul van de Kooi Kitchens. Emperador marble with a stainless-steel strip along the front.

Cupboard interiors in glued birch multiplex and façades in three-layer oak laminate, in a wengé colour.

A Wolf cooker (width: 173 cm) and a Sub Zero fridge-freezer combination (width: 122 cm).

Viking wine racks and a Homemade extractor.

The work surface in this kitchen was cast on-site in concrete. Cupboard interiors in glued birch multiplex; façades and sides in three-layer "rustic brown" oak laminate.

An open fireplace with a surround, Itho extractor, a Miele high-pressure steam oven and a warming drawer.

PAUL VAN DE KOOI

Heliumweg 40a

NL – 3812 RE Amersfoort

T +31 (0)33 465 11 11

F +31 (0)33 465 11 77

www.paulvandekooi.nl

info@paulvandekooi.nl

Cooker (width: 92 cm) and fridge/freezer (width: 122 cm) by Viking.

FUNCTIONALITY WITH A CONTEMPORARY ATMOSPHERE

De Menagerie is one of the leading traditional kitchen-construction companies in the Low Countries.

All of the company's designs are custom-made and installed by the De Menagerie team.

Even though every project is created completely from scratch, this company from Aalst always maintains the same high standards, motivated by a passion for perfect design and finish, based on the exclusive use of durable materials.

For each new assignment De Menagerie devises a concept that works in harmony with the space, with functionality and aesthetics going hand in hand.

Both De Menagerie's country-style projects and more contemporary kitchens are reduced to their essence, and characterised by their timeless feel and warm atmosphere.

This kitchen furniture is in MDF, clad with oak veneer with a natural finish.

The steel handles are custom-made accessories.

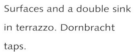

Surfaces and a double sink in terrazzo. Dornbracht taps.

p.48
Oven and hob by Viking and an American bottom-mount refrigerator by Amana.
The built-in Miele steam oven is concealed behind sliding doors.

DE MENAGERIE
   Leo de Bethunelaan 45
   B – 9300 Aalst
   T +32 (0)53 78 69 39
   F +32 (0)53 70 79 96
   www.demenagerie.be
   info@demenagerie.be

TURNKEY SOLUTIONS

Home Design offers turnkey solutions for every renovation project: from kitchen design (by a team of experienced interior architects) to construction and finish, with a building contractor to take care of every stage of the construction or renovation process, including electricity, plumbing, carpentry, floors and paintwork.

As well as kitchens, which are one of Home Design's specialities, this Brussels company is also extremely skilled in creating and constructing exclusive bathrooms, dressing rooms, cloakrooms, and so on, up to and including the complete coordination of renovation projects: from the structural work to the smallest finishing detail.

The Home Design showroom is available to help clients with the selection of materials, the presentation of furniture and lighting (Luz and XVL tables, Meridiani seating, S. Davidts lighting) and with inspiration for the creation of the complete interior.

The kitchen furniture is in bleached and brushed oak, protected with a matt varnish. Work surface in Rustenburg Dark, a South African variety of granite, in an Anciento finish.

The sinks are built from Rustenburg granite.

HOME DESIGN
avenue de Hinnisdael 14B
B – 1150 Brussels
T +32 (0)2 771 99 10
F +32 (0)2 770 78 85
www.homedesign .be
home.design@skynet.be

A Smeg cooker with two ovens.

The Amana refrigerator in stainless steel and coloured glass has been integrated into the ceiling-height wall unit.

THE TIMELESS POWER
OF SOLID WOOD WITHIN
A STREAMLINED DESIGN

Tack Kitchens and Furniture devise and create functional, top-quality design: furniture and custom-made work that push the technical boundaries, in a timeless, yet contemporary style.

The company respects the natural colour and appearance of the wood used. Tack's creations are unique and are further enhanced by the research into materials, colour and light that the company carries out.
Every project demonstrates a strong sense of symmetry and balanced proportions.

p. 56 & 58-59

Pull-out units have been used throughout this kitchen design.

Tack was also the consultant for colour, light and decoration. The work of art harmonises with the style and shades of the kitchen. The chairs are a Tack design.

Vertical lighting within the cooker canopy lends an additional dimension to this streamlined design.

The work surfaces and sinks, which are at an ideal working height, are in an exclusive white veined marble.

The teppan yaki, or grill plate, is built into the table and also has a warming function. The hand-operated hatch provides lots of storage space.

TACK
Kitchens and furniture: design and creation

> Grotstraat 71
> B – 8780 Oostrozebeke
> T +32 (0)51 40 47 18
> F +32 (0)51 40 61 40
>
> Menenstraat 472
> B – 8560 Wevelgem
> T +32 (0)56 42 50 95
>
> www.tack-keukens.be
> info@tack-keukens.be

p. 62-63

A kitchen in aged dark pin oak in combination with matt pearl-grey.

The seating blocks also provide storage space.

The wall unit with built-in appliances is operated electrically.

The dishwasher is in a practical position on the front of the central unit.

An unusual beige natural stone has been selected for the unit's work surface and ledge.

The ledge conceals the sink area and has the tap fixed to it.

The pull-out cooker hood is a technical innovation.

A solid sheet of pin oak has been incorporated into the natural-stone surface and is used as a dining area.

THE KITCHEN AS
THE CENTRE OF THE HOME

Mape is a family concern that has specialised in the production of kitchens and bathroom furniture for over forty years. The architecture, ergonomics and functionality of the kitchen are at the heart of every project: the kitchen is an essential element of the living environment.

All of the lacquering work is carried out in the company's own workshops and is of the highest quality.

The extensive kitchen range can be selected in different materials: from MDF with a high-gloss or matt finish to solid natural or synthetic materials. All of the kitchens are developed by Mape's design team from the basic plan to create a unique design that corresponds perfectly to the wishes of the client.

A streamlined kitchen in MDF with a white matt finish and no door furniture.

The central island is equipped with a rectangular sink and Dornbracht taps, and is also used as a table: it can seat four people.

The contrast of the dark oak floor with the white units and walls lends a sober and serene appearance to this kitchen.

The work surface is in lava stone.

The alcove containing the cooking surface has sliding doors. These cupboards provide practical storage space for small pieces of electrical equipment.

The positioning of the three Atag ovens at the same height reinforces the streamlined look of the kitchen.

This custom-made kitchen is in solid aged oak. The doors have no handles and are built from three layers of material for optimal stability.

The Amana refrigerator has been completely integrated into the wall unit. The wood grain runs horizontally on the drawers and pull-out cupboards, emphasising the impression of length. All of the drawers and pull-out cupboards are equipped with fully telescopic, silent runners.

The work surface, in harmony with the large floor tiles, is in 5cm-thick smoothed bluestone, with two square sinks in the same material. Taps by Dornbracht. The cooking area consists of a flat induction plate and an extractor built into the plain MDF canopy, which has been painted to match the ceiling.

MAPE nv
    Baardegemstraat 13
    B – 9420 Erpe-Mere
    T +32 (0)53 60 30 60
    F +32 (0)53 63 09 23
    www.mape.be
    info@mape.be

A PASSION FOR DESIGN
AND FINE QUALITY

Driven by a passion for techniques and home interiors, the De Keyzer family has been producing kitchens with pure and timeless designs for thirty years.

Creativity and craftsmanship are at the centre of all of their projects: the additional selling points of this kitchen-design company are the luxurious details and the incomparable finish.

A bold, modern design with the appeal of a loft.

The white-lacquered high-gloss doors create a fresh contrast with the impressive work surface.

All mod cons are present, including induction hobs, a pyrolysis oven and a cooker hood, ingeniously hidden from view.

The cooking and washing-up island is a central point that allows free and easy circulation.

The stainless-steel work surfaces create a beautiful, semi-industrial feel. Combined with the moss-green tint of the oak, this results in a warm and timeless look.

Woodworking requires a great deal of know-how. De Keyzer has specialised in flawless carpentry for thirty years and can guarantee hardwearing perfection.

The fine façades have been professionally treated so that they are very easy to take care of.

The outstanding quality and beautiful finish can be seen in even the smallest details.

DE KEYZER
Kitchen architecture
    Industrielaan 55
    B – 8930 Menen
    T +32 (0)56 52 13 40
    F +32 (0)56 52 13 41
    www.dekeyzer.be
    info@dekeyzer.be

    Shop Sint-Martens-Latem
    Kortrijksesteenweg 1
    B – 9830 Sint-Martens-Latem

A PURE PHILOSOPHY FOR KITCHEN AND HOME DESIGN

In his dedicated search for manufacturers who could develop his ideas with a great deal of care and a high-quality finish, industrial designer Ivo de Groot found the Italian company Strato.

Since then, Ivo de Groot has been the exclusive Strato distributor for Belgium. Strato's techniques and choice of materials were so close to his requirements that it was only logical that they should enter into a close collaboration.

Ivo de Groot and Marco Gorini have been Strato's regular design team ever since.

Their passion for kitchens has expanded in recent years to become a total vision of interior design.
Since 2005, their home-design philosophy has been on display in a magnificent show-room on Ernest Van Dijckkaai in Antwerp.
Strato Casa have a number of pieces in their regular collection, but on request they also create custom-made furniture that is completely in keeping with the Strato range.

The façades of this Strato kitchen are in bleached oak veneer.

The details in this kitchen are
finished in stainless steel.

Work surfaces and floors in Monte Dura natural stone.

The Strato concept applied to an open kitchen and dining area.

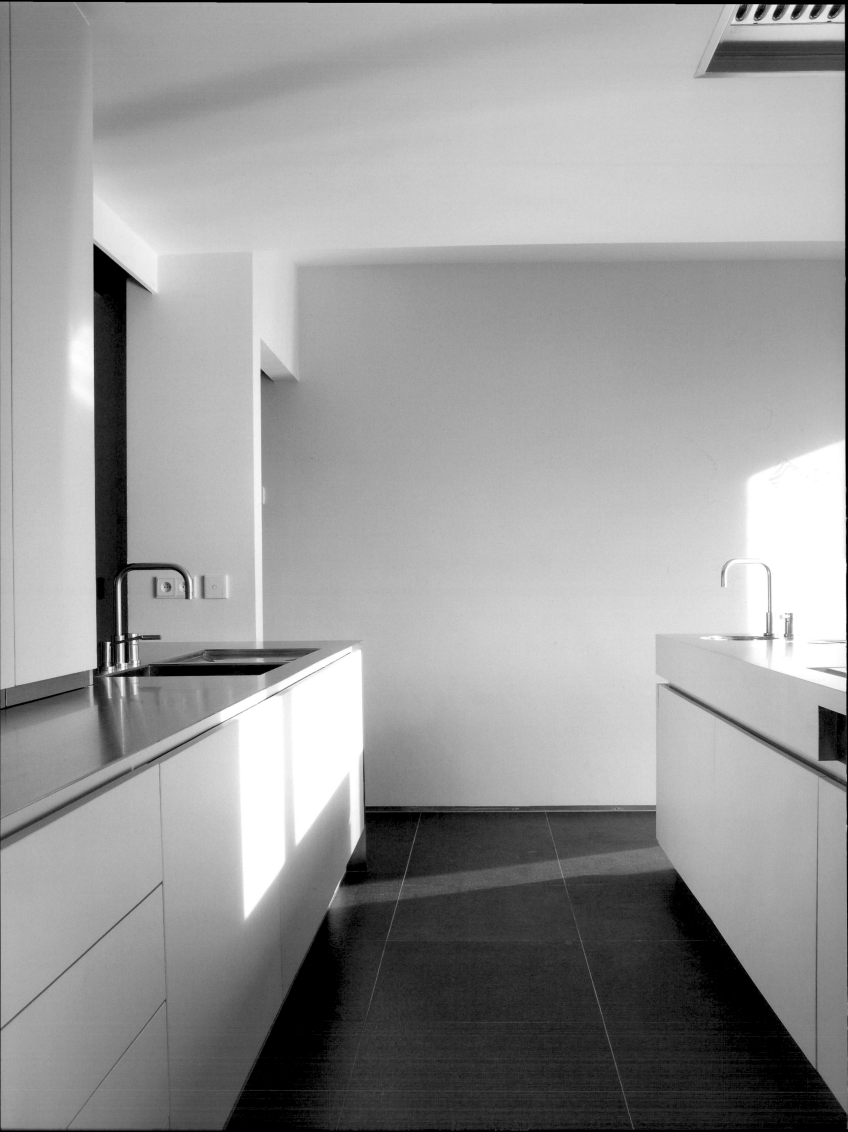

This kitchen was created by Ivo de Groot in close collaboration with the Brussels architect Dao Le-Nhu.

Façades in light-grey "stratocolor" (the company's own solid-core laminate). The work surfaces are in stainless steel with a satinised finish. Sides in stratocolor.

IVO DE GROOT bvba
Exclusive STRATO distributor for Belgium
E. Van Dijckkaai 7
B – 2000 Antwerpen
T +32 (0)3 248 27 37
F +32 (0)3 248 27 36
www.stratobelgium.com

Façades in white stratocolor. The work surface in the kitchen area and the sides of the central unit are in Scotchbrite stainless steel. The surface and façades of the central unit are in white stratocolor.

THE HIGHEST QUALITY
AS STANDARD

For over fifty years, Wilfra ID & E have created kitchens and interiors in their own familiar style.

A passion for details, sophistication and architecture is combined with an almost fanatical degree of craftsmanship in which the highest quality is standard. A team of interior architects, technicians and finishers works with the clients to create a living environment that corresponds to all of their wishes and specifications.

Together with his 22 staff members, Stephen Fraeye, the head of the company, feels the pulse of the market, creates trends and translates these into tangible living projects at home and abroad.
The projects presented here are perfect evidence of this process.

This project involves the thorough renovation of a kitchen.

To make the kitchen appear larger and create a sense of depth, an alcove has been cut into the rear wall. The work surface extends into the alcove, creating an extra dimension.

This kitchen has been designed with very clean
lines and simple, natural and stylish materials.
The work surface and wall are clad with greige
Buxy. Doors in fine oak stained veneer.
The paintwork is in restful white.

WILFRA ID & E

    Henri Lebbestraat 178

    B – 8790 Waregem

    T +32 (0)56 61 21 61

    F +32 (0)56 61 23 69

    www.wilfra.be

    info@wilfra.be

This kitchen was created for a Dutch-American couple.

The floor is in Carrara marble and the work surfaces are Corian. The façades are
in specially selected American walnut with a wonderful repeating grain,
beautifully bookmatched over a length of 10 metres.

The door has been perfectly integrated. Gaggenau equipment and a wok ring
under a Corian lid. This is a majestic kitchen in which all of the details are
absolutely right.

AN ENVIABLE REPUTATION

Arcade Kitchens owes its enviable reputation to its custom-made kitchens and the turnkey concept.

Annick van der Wolf, the founder of Arcade, has always devised her exclusive kitchen designs with a great sense of creativity.

Arcade's construction of high-quality kitchens, which are entirely custom-made, is perfectly in keeping with the style of the classic "cottage" kitchen, but this company from Brabant walloon also includes quite a number of contemporary designs on its list of achievements.

Arcade can even take care of the complete renovation and fitting-out of the kitchen space.

This kitchen, designed by Annick van der Wolf, features an interplay of black and white contrasts and stainless steel.
Doors in wood veneer, tinted black.
The work surface and the table are in 6cm-thick stainless steel. A rhythmic and linear succession of columns, false ceilings and the kitchen unit, which extends into the table.

ARCADE

Avenue Comte d'Ursel 38
B - 1390 Grez-Doiceau (Wavre)
T +32 (0)10 84 15 05
F +32 (0)10 84 05 36
www.arcadecuisine.be
info@arcadecuisine.be
Open Monday to Friday
from 1.30 to 6.00.
Saturday from 10.00 to 5.00
or by appointment.

This kitchen was created using ivory-white matt and gloss doors.

The work surface is in Quartz Compac (colour: Luna).

HORIZONTALITY
AND CLEAR-CUT LINES

Olivier Dwek, in collaboration with Julie Ruquois, created this contemporary kitchen design during the renovation of a villa in the leafy outskirts of Brussels.

The sense of horizontality and the simple interplay of lines have been accentuated by the furniture selected and by the long glass section providing a view of the garden.

The plasma screen is fitted to a wall finished in blackboard paint.
Lithos switches in a charcoal finish.

Slate surfaces with solid sink basins carved out from the stone. The cooking hobs and the extractor are situated on the central island.

The tall stainless-steel unit containing the refrigerator and storage space was designed as a freestanding block, and has access to the dining room on either side.

Aluminium bar stools from the Emeco collection designed by Starck (at Instore).

OLIVIER DWEK
Consultancy for architecture and interior architecture
Brugmannlaan 34
B – 1060 Brussels
T +32 (0)2 344 28 04
F +32 (0)2 344 28 00
MOB +32 (0)475 666 100
dwek.architectes@gmail.com

SOBER SOPHISTICATION

Sober sophistication: this description perfectly captures the style of Obumex.

In 1960, the company started to design and create custom-made kitchens in which technological know-how and an unfailing sense of style go hand in hand. These are kitchens and complete living environments that have effortlessly withstood the test of time with their revolutionary designs and the consistent use of hardwearing, distinctive materials.

p. 126-133
Obumex created this project to a design by architect Stephanie Laporte of 'The Office Belgium'.

The architect went for a sober design, but used contrasting materials, such as dark tinted wood and heavily veined marble. It was most important for the client that the kitchen should have all mod cons, yet remain easy to use and child-friendly.

The result is a contemporary kitchen, which is timeless in its subtle shades and its sober design.

NE DEMANDE PAS TROP
CONTENTE TOI DE PEU

The cooking block is made from dark tinted oak veneer with concealed handles, clad with Emperador natural stone. The dining table and coach were designed by Stephanie Laporte, custom-made in matt lacquer. Illumination: light channel with white Lotis fittings. Cotto d'Este floor.

OBUMEX
Showroom Staden
        Diksmuidestraat 121
        B - 8840 Staden
        T +32 (0)51 70 50 71
        F +32 (0)51 70 50 81
Showroom Antwerp
        L. de Waelplaats 20
        B - 2000 Antwerp
        T +32 (0)3 238 00 30
Showroom Brussels
        Waterloolaan 30
        B - 1000 Brussels
        T +32 (0)2 502 97 80
Showroom Knokke
        Sparrendreef 83
        B - 8300 Knokke
        T +32 (0)50 601 666
        www.obumex.be
        design@obumex.be

p 134-135
This project by
Obumex aims for a
cooler atmosphere:
white lacquer,
stainless steel,
Basaltina stone and
pearl-grey veneer.

CREATIVE CRAFTMANSHIP

Simply designing a kitchen is not enough: the design has to be functional, aesthetically pleasing and distinctive into the bargain.
With over fifteen years of experience, interior architects Mr. and Mrs. Van Havere–de Hasque and their son Xavier design kitchens that perfectly fulfil all of these criteria.

The functional and practical aspects of the kitchen, the use of the space, the friendly atmosphere and the view are all of equal importance. At Ambiance Cuisine, good design is essential and has to respect the lifestyle and requirements of each individual client: washing and preparation areas, space for cooking and eating, storage... and a place where the whole family can come together.

The Ambiance Cuisine team takes care of not only the kitchen design, but also all of the work and installation. They recommend a contractor for every stage of the building or renovation process and then the company's fitters, with over twenty years of experience under their belts, get to work: they guarantee the smooth operation and perfect installation of your dream kitchen.

Once more, the Ambiance Cuisine team has combined the warmth of wood with purist lines.

The tops have been made of a rare African granite, mixed with stainless steel colums.

The appliances are from the famous Gaggenau brand.

This kitchen is by Poggenpohl, the German kitchen manufacturer whom ambiance Cuisine represents in Brussels for more than fifteen years now.

AMBIANCE CUISINE

  Chaussée de Waterloo 1138
  B – 1180 Brussels
  T +32 (0)2 375 24 36

AMBIANCE CUISINE

  Avenue Reine Astrid 479-481
  B – 1950 Kraainem
  T +32 (0)2 767 12 17

  www.ambiancecuisine.com

  Open from Tuesday to Friday
  from 10.00 to 1.00
  and from 2.00 to 6.00.
  Saturday from 10.00 to 6.00.

This Gaggenau cooking ensemble with domino grill, ceramic glass hob and deep fryer is the result of a detailed study carried out by the team of interior architects from Ambiance Cuisine. The professional extractor is custom-made. The steam oven, the microwave and the oven are by Miele. The stainless-steel work surface has been given a special patina treatment.
The originality of this kitchen comes from the combination of stainless steel and cerused wood for the central section. Fonte-Paffoni taps (model: stick professional).

A PASSION
FOR THE OPEN KITCHEN

Fahrenheit is a kitchen designer and distributor of exclusive cookers and kitchen accessories. The company is based in Brussels and directed by Thierry Goffin, the founder of Fahrenheit.

All kitchens created by Fahrenheit exhibit the same attention to durability, selection of fine materials and perfect finish.

The projects in this report perfectly demonstrate the company's passion for uncompromising quality.

The kitchen in this large house from the 1950s was provided for the domestic staff. The current owner had the original idea of transforming one of the garages into a large kitchen and dining area for the whole family. Simple oak planks were chosen for the furniture, in harmony with the Azul Cascais natural stone. The cooking island contains a Lacanche cooker and a "bergerie" oven in which a whole lamb can be cooked. The custom-made cooker hood in glass and stainless steel was designed by Thierry Goffin.

The wall separating the kitchen from the second garage is fully panelled in solid oak, interrupted only by an open fireplace at grill height. The wall also contains storage space and the door to the garage.

p. 146-149

The challenge in this rather small apartment consisted of designing an entirely new kitchen in the middle of the living room, thereby allowing an extra room to be created in the space where the previous kitchen had been.

Furniture in dark-tinted oak for the island and painted MDF in the same colours as the walls for the cupboard units. The false ceiling serves as an extractor unit and has a built-in extraction system. This means that the extractor is kept out of sight, yet functions efficiently. Such ingenious details ensure that this room looks more like a friendly bar than just a kitchen.

Three wine refrigerators mean that these wine lovers do not have to keep visiting the cellar, which is six floors down. The units also serve as a sideboard.

Work surfaces in specially selected, extra-white Carrara marble, as is the sink unit, which has been discreetly incorporated into the cupboard with sliding doors.

The kitchen has been concealed in this contemporary duplex apartment and integrated into a living space that includes a concert piano, huge sofas and a large plasma screen.

These work surfaces are made from MDF painted in a fondant-chocolate shade, topped with taupe natural stone from Charles Kreglinger.

This simple and warm sandstone harmonises perfectly with the furniture and is also acid-proof. The wall lights create the impression of a library: only the cooker serves as a reminder that this is a kitchen.

p. 154-157

This kitchen is situated in the dining room of a sumptuous house in Brussels. The owners, who are from London, wanted a spectacular, almost completely black kitchen. The furniture, the Viking cooker, the work surfaces and the Moroccan zeliges are all in gloss black. The only exceptions to this rule are the sand-coloured floor and the stainless steel refrigerator.

FAHRENHEIT

avenue Louise 130 b
B – 1050 Brussels
TEL.: +32 (0)2 644 28 00
FAX: +32 (0)2 644 27 87
www.fahrenheit.be
fahrenheit@fahrenheit.be

PART II

EXCLUSIVE MATERIALS AND KITCHEN WARE

A SPECIALIST IN HIGH-QUALITY KITCHEN WORK SURFACES

At the beginning of 2007, the family concern of Louis Culot moved to a brand-new base in Ruisbroek (Puurs) after over 75 years in Londerzeel.

This new headquarters gives the dynamic supplier of natural stone the necessary room for expansion: the floor space has almost doubled, from 2500 to 4500 square metres. The offices, showroom and natural-stone workshops have all been accommodated within the new industrial premises.

Over the years, Louis Culot has become a real niche player, concentrating exclusively on the manufacture of high-quality work surfaces in granite, limestone and composite. Louis Culot is one of the best-equipped and most technologically advanced natural-stone suppliers on the Belgian market: computer-controlled CNC machines allow the firm to offer durable work surfaces for competitive prices and within a reasonable period of time.

Louis Culot, the head of the company, and his son Tim have the ambition of making their company one of the major players within the Benelux market: they already supply hundreds of kitchen work surfaces every year to kitchen producers and private clients throughout Belgium and part of Luxembourg.
The rapid growth that Louis Culot's natural-stone company has experienced in recent years will undoubtedly continue in the new company premises.

p. 160 & 162-163

The work surfaces in this kitchen, designed and created by Devaere sa, were made in white Carrara marble by Louis Culot, with a smoothed finish, and mitred to give a thickness of 5 cm.

The work surfaces in this kitchen project were created by Louis Culot in "Misty Caramel" composite stone by Diresco, and mitred to give a thickness of 6 cm.

LOUIS CULOT bvba
Natural-stone suppliers
    Industriezone Pullaar
    Schoonmansveld 7
    B – 2870 Puurs
    T +32 (0)3 860 70 70
    F +32 (0)3 860 70 79
    www.culot.be
    info@culot.be

TOP SUPPLIERS
OF EXCLUSIVE COOKERS
AND KITCHEN EQUIPMENT

The Ghent company Adek was founded in 1980 and within a quarter of a century has become one of the leading distributors of top-quality cookers and other kitchen equipment in the Benelux countries.

Adek displays and supplies cookers from major manufacturers such as Delaubrac, Viking, Esse, Morice, Lacanche, Mercury, Cucineria, Smeg, Rosières, Metal Industries Lyon, La Cornue and others.

For customers who are looking for powerful, but quiet extractor systems, Adek usually suggests a custom-made cooker hood. Different types of motor can be combined with built-in systems and pullout cooker hoods or decorative extractor chimneys.

The company's range of exclusive refrigerators and storage units is also impressive, including models by Sub Zero, Norcool, Amana, Festivo, Liebherr, Eurocave, Müller, U-Line, General Electric and Smeg.

Finally, Adek also supplies built-in appliances for the kitchen, selecting only the very best for their showroom: Gaggenau, Küppersbusch, Miele, Imperial, Neff, Siemens, Mercury, Novy, Kitchenaid, Fisher & Paykel, Magimix, Lavazza, Bamix – a most varied selection with one common factor: the absolute top quality and exclusivity of every make.

At Adek there are unusual cookers and appliances that can be found in only very few places. It is most definitely worth paying a visit to the showroom in Sint-Amandsberg (near Ghent).

This kitchen was designed by Van Ransbeeck Totaalinterieur.

The cooker is an all-electric Cucineria Royal 130, with an oven and warming compartment, four ceramic zones and an electric grill.

Adek presents only top-quality appliances: a Sub Zero 632S side-by-side refrigerator, a Wolf gas cooktop, a custom-made cooker hood, a Quooker instant boiling-water tap, an Irinox water dispenser and (below on this page) an Irinox Blast Chiller / Shock Freddy.

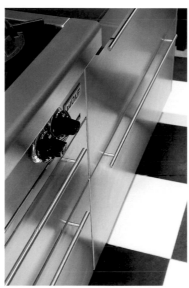

ADEK

Grondwetlaan 81
B – 9040 Gent (Sint-Amandsberg)
T +32 (0)9 251 49 99
F +32 (0)9 251 65 64
Showroom opening hours:
Tuesday to Friday
from 1.00 to 6.00.
Saturday from 10.00 to 12.00
and 1.30 to 5.00.

www.adek.be
info@adek.be

THE COOKER
AS THE HEART OF THE KITCHEN

For over a quarter of a century, Alfa Belgium has been the exclusive importer of the legendary Aga cookers in Belgium and Luxembourg.

Some time ago, the company also became the exclusive distributor for Falcon in Belgium and Luxembourg.
The first Falcon cooker was made in 1833. Five generations of experts have made this cooker into a bestseller. In 2007, Alfa Belgium/Alfa Bis is placing the focus on three Falcon designs: the "Classic Deluxe", the "Excel" and the "Deluxe CT".

Alfa Belgium also won the right a few years ago to import the top-quality French La Cornue cookers into Belgium: this was a new development for this family company from Ghent, which within twenty-five years has become the port of call for advice on all three top-quality brands of cooker.

The robust Aga cooker can also be integrated very well within a contemporary kitchen environment.

This exceptional kitchen and dining area, created by the Brussels kitchen designer Fahrenheit, illustrates this perfectly.

The works of art featuring roosters are by Philippe Schlienger.

Château La Cornue is a prestigious range of legendary cookers, exclusively custom-made to order in a wide variety of colours and finishes.

CornuFé is a new range in the La Cornue family: robust, functional and timeless.

Falcon is a subsidiary of Aga and aims for the same high standards of production and quality. Falcon cookers are available in a variety of colours.

The three new star cookers of the Falcon range: the Classic Deluxe, the Excel and the Deluxe CT.

ALFA BELGIUM nv / ALFA BIS bvba

Showroom:
Nijverheidskaai 2
B – 9040 Gent
T +32 (0)9 228 14 84
F +32 (0)9 228 06 13
www.aga.be
info@aga.be
www.falconkookfornuizen.be
www.lacornue.fr

WESTAHL: NEW TO
THE CONTEMPORARY KITCHEN

As the exclusive Belgian importer of Lacanche cookers, Abel Falisse has also recently started recommending the "modern design" version: Westahl.

Westahl cookers are produced in the Lacanche factories to the same high standards of quality, but with a decidedly contemporary look: stainless steel in a streamlined design that has been reduced to its absolute essence.
Its appearance raises high expectations, which are completely satisfied by the cooker's performance. These are genuine semi-professional cookers, which can also be adapted to the individual specifications of every customer: widths of 70 to 150 cm, with every imaginable type of oven (conventional or convection ovens, single or double ones, gas or electric, with or without a grill and warming cabinet).

Westahl provides perfectly planned modular cooking solutions for the modern design aficionado and gourmet.

The cooking surface of the WRG 1540 by Westahl can be tailored to the customer's own specifications.

The WCF 1052 GE model with a simmer plate and four gas burners, a gas oven and an electric one.

All of the important equipment can be stored under the cooking surface, allowing perfect and flexible organisation.

The hob units can be electric or even induction hobs.
Above, with a fryer and a lavastone grill.

Subtle colours to harmonise with the stainless-steel look of the Westahl: models ranging from seventy centimetres wide to a metre and a half, in anthracite, armor, mastic, mandarin, silice green and stainless steel.

The smallest Westahl model is 70 centimetres wide. Here in pearl white, Chinese red, mandarin and warm grey.

Ets. ABEL FALISSE sa
(Exclusive importer)
T +32 (0)4 252 71 73
F +32 (0)4 252 12 79
www.abel-falisse.be
Info@abel-falisse.be
(Showroom in Brussels on appointment)

ADDRESSES

Ets. ABEL FALISSE sa
(Exclusive importer)
T +32 (0)4 252 71 73
F +32 (0)4 252 12 79
www.abel-falisse.be
Info@abel-falisse.be
p. 184-189

ADEK
Grondwetlaan 81
B – 9040 Gent (Sint-Amandsberg)
T +32 (0)9 251 49 99
F +32 (0)9 251 65 64
Opening hours showroom:
Monday to Friday, 1 to 6 PM.
On Saturday from 10 to 12 and 1.30 to 5 PM
www.adek.be
info@adek.be
P. 168-173

ALFA BELGIUM / ALFA BIS
Showroom:
Nijverheidskaai 2
B – 9040 Gent
T +32 (0)9 228 14 84
F +32 (0)9 228 06 13
www.aga.be
info@aga.be
www.falconkookfornuizen.be
www.lacornue.fr
p. 174-183

AMBIANCE CUISINE
Chaussée de Waterloo 1138
B – 1180 Brussels
T +32 (0)2 375 24 36
AMBIANCE CUISINE
Avenue Reine Astrid 479-481
B – 1950 Kraainem
T +32 (0)2 767 12 17
www.ambiancecuisine.com
Open Tuesday to Friday
from 10 to 1 and from 2 to 6.
Saturdays from 10 to 6.
P. 136-141

ARCADE
Avenue Comte d'Ursel 38
B - 1390 Grez-Doiceau (Wavre)
T +32 (0)10 84 15 05
F +32 (0)10 84 05 36
www.arcadecuisine.be
info@arcadecuisine.be
Open Monday to Friday from 1.30 to 6.
Saturdays from 10 to 5 or on appointment.
p. 114-119

BAUDOUIN COURTENS
Architect
av. Napoléon 152/2
B – 1180 Brussels
T +32 (0)2 375 35 12
F +32 (0)2 375 29 41
www.courtens.be
bc@courtens.be
p. 24-29

p. 192-193
A project by
De Menagerie.

p. 194
An Olivier Dwek
concept.

CULOT LOUIS sprl
Natural stone
Industriezone Pullaar
Schoonmansveld 7
B – 2870 Puurs
T +32 (0)3 860 70 70
www.culot.be
info@culot.be
P. 160-167

DE KEYZER
Kitchen Architecture
Industrielaan 55
B – 8930 Menen
T +32 (0)56 52 13 40
F +32 (0)56 52 13 41
www.dekeyzer.be
info@dekeyzer.be
Shop Sint-Martens-Latem
Kortrijksesteenweg 1
B – 9830 Sint-Martens-Latem
p. 74-91

DE MENAGERIE
Leo de Bethunelaan 45
B – 9300 Aalst
T +32 (0)53 78 69 39
F +32 (0)53 70 79 96
www.demenagerie.be
info@demenagerie.be
p. 46-51

DWEK OLIVIER
Architects and interior Architecture
avenue Brugmann 34
B – 1060 Brussels
T +32 (0)2 344 28 04
F +32 (0)2 344 28 00
MOB +32 (0)475 666 100
dwek.architectes@gmail.com
p. 120-125

FAHRENHEIT
avenue Louise 130 b
B – 1050 Brussels
T +32 (0)2 644 28 00
F +32 (0)2 644 27 87
www.fahrenheit.be
fahrenheit@fahrenheit.be
P. 142-157

HOME DESIGN
avenue de Hinnisdael 14B
B – 1150 Woluwe-Saint-Pierre
T +32 (0)2 771 99 10
F +32 (0)2 770 78 85
www.homedesign .be
home.design@skynet.be
p. 52-55

IVO DE GROOT sprl
Exclusive STRATO distributor for Belgium
E. Van Dijckkaai 7
B – 2000 Antwerpen
T +32 (0)3 248 27 37
F +32 (0)3 248 27 36
www.stratobelgium.com
p. 92-105

MAPE nv
Baardegemstraat 13
B – 9420 Erpe-Mere
T +32 (0)53 60 30 60
F +32 (0)53 63 09 23
www.mape .be
info@mape.be
p. 64-73

p. 196
A project by Devaere
sa. Tops in Carrara
marble by Louis Culot.

OBUMEX
Showroom Staden
Diksmuidestraat 121
B - 8840 Staden
T +32 (0)51 70 50 71
F +32 (0)51 70 50 81
Showroom Anvers
L. de Waelplaats 20
B - 2000 Anvers
TEL.: +32 (0)3 238 00 30
Showroom Bruxelles
Waterloolaan 30
B - 1000 Bruxelles
TEL.: +32 (0)2 502 97 80
Showroom Knokke
Sparrendreef 83
B - 8300 Knokke
T +32 (0)50 601 666
www.obumex.be
design@obumex.be
p. 126-135

OFFICE BELGIUM (The)
Stephanie Laporte
Doorniksewijk 49
B – 8500 Kortrijk
T +32 (0)56 326 108
F +32 (0)56 326 109
laporte.partners@telenet.be
p. 126-133

TACK
Concept and production
Grotstraat 74
B – 8780 Oostrozebeke
T +32 (0)51 40 47 18
F +32 (0)51 40 61 40
Menenstraat 472
B – 8560 Wevelgem
T +32 (0)56 42 50 95
www.tack-keukens.be
info@tack-keukens.be
p. 56-63

PAUL VAN DE KOOI
Heliumweg 40a
NL – 3812 RE Amersfoort
T +31 (0)33 465 11 11
F +31 (0)33 465 11 77
www.paulvandekooi.nl
info@paulvandekooi.nl
p. 30-45

VAN RAVESTYN sprl
Architect
Kastelein 70
B – 2300 Turnhout
T +32 (0)14 42 77 41
F +32 (0)14 43 77 44
www.vanravestyn.be
info@vanravestyn.be
p. 16-23

WILFRA ID & E
Henri Lebbestraat 178
B – 8790 Waregem
T +32 (0)56 61 21 61
F +32 (0)56 61 23 69
www.wilfra.be
info@wilfra.be
p. 106-113

p. 198
A project by architect
Van Ravestyn.

p. 200-201
A kitchen by
De Menagerie.

PUBLISHER
BETA-PLUS Publishing
Termuninck 3
B - 7850 Enghien (Belgium)
T +32 (0)2 395 90 20
F +32 (0)2 395 90 21
www.betaplus.com
betaplus@skynet.be

PHOTOGRAPHY
All pictures: Jo Pauwels, except for 187-188 Abel Falisse.

GRAPHIC DESIGN
POLYDEM
Nathalie Binart

TRANSLATION
Laura Watkinson

January 2007
ISBN 13: 978 90 772 1371 1
ISBN 10: 90 772 1371 6